# THE PATH

# TO PURPOSE

## FOLLOWING THE
## PRINCIPLES OF GOD

## Tranisha LeShawn

SC Publications

Beaumont, Texas, USA

PUBLICATIONS

**The Path to Purpose**

Following the Principles of God  Copyright © 2025

ISBN: 979-8-9928077-0-7 (Paperback)

ISBN: 979-8-9928077-2-1 (ebook)

Library of Congress Control Number 2025904947


Author name: Tranisha LeShawn, 1984

Title: The Path to Purpose: Following the Principles of God

First Edition


Published by: SC Publications

Imprint: SC Publications

Address:3195 Dowlen Rd, Ste 101-386 Beaumont, TX 77706

Email: purposewriting@sufficientlycovered.com

Website: www.sufficientlycovered.com

SC
PUBLICATIONS

Unless indicated otherwise, all scripture quotations are taken from the King James Version of the Holy Bible.

# DEDICATIONS

This book is dedicated to my leaders, Chief Apostle J. Garcia and Pastor B. Simon. Thank you for the daily advice, agape love, and servitude to God and his workings. Your teachings under the direction of the Holy Spirit do not go unnoticed. Inspiration for this book comes not only from God but also through your teachings. Thank you for loving me unconditionally and being examples of how to live a life pleasing to God. Thank you for teaching me to let go and let God have his way in my life. Thank you for supporting me in everything I do in every way you could. I love you both very much!

Dedicated to all who aspire to be above average and want to walk in their Purpose.

You can do it!

*If you put God first, you will succeed!*

*If you follow God's path, you will succeed!*

*If you put your Faith and trust in God, you will succeed!*

*If you persist, you will succeed!*

# ACKNOWLEDGEMENTS

**P**rimarily, I give all thanks to my Heavenly Father. Without him, there would be no inspiration for me. I thank God for always being there, especially when I didn't know where to turn. I honor God for allowing me to create this book, along with the others, to be a blessing to his people and myself.

Thank you to my church family, Miracles in Motion World Wide Ministries, and New Covenant Global Empowerment Ministry (Women's Department).

To my daddy, my big guy, Lawrence Harkless, your presence is greatly missed, I can still hear your encouraging words and will cherish your memory forever.

*To my big sister and friend Tracy Armstead. This book has been a long time in the making and I still hear you fussing at me to get it done! Thank you for the push, fussing, love, and unconditional support in getting this book completed!! You have been a real blessing to me; I love you!*

# TABLE OF CONTENT

# INTRODUCTION

**W**here do I turn? What direction do I take? Is this the right thing to do? Am I making the best decision? I hope I can do this. If this doesn't work out, I can just do something else. What if this does work out? What if it doesn't? Who can I ask for help? Who can give me the best advice? Who should I partner with? Should I get a partner? Will I be successful? Should I go back? Should I even start? How do I know this will even work? What if everyone mocks me? What if no one supports me? How will I get the money? These, among many others, are questions we often ask ourselves when we want to make a new decision. Oftentimes, we turn to the wrong people for advice. Some may have the best intentions for us, but the best advice-giver is God. He knows the plans that he has laid out for our lives. He knows what path we should take to succeed and prosper in everything we do. Our friends can only give us so much, and often we leave still needing answers.

In this book, *The Path to Purpose*, we will explore how to align your life with God's principles and discover the unique purpose He has for you. This journey is not about perfection or having all the answers right away. It's about learning to trust God, even when the path ahead seems unclear. It's about adjusting your mindset, writing down your vision, and taking actionable steps toward the life God has called you to live.

I've been where you are—filled with questions, doubts, and fears. But through prayer, faith, and a willingness to let God lead, I've seen how He can transform uncertainty into clarity and fear into confidence. My hope is that this book will serve as a guide for you, just as it has been and still is for me, as you navigate your own path to purpose.

As you read, I encourage you to reflect on your own life. What are the areas where you feel stuck? Where do you need God's guidance the most? Take notes, pray over the scriptures, and allow God to speak to you through these pages. Remember, your purpose is not just about what you do—it's about who you are in Christ and how you can bring glory to Him through your life.

Let's begin this journey together. Let's discover what it means to walk in purpose, on purpose.

# CHAPTER 1

# WHO'S LEADING WHO?

**W**ho is the leader in your life? Are you leading yourself? Are you allowing your surroundings to lead you? Are you allowing God to take the reigns and lead you? Who is first in your life? These are crucial questions to ask, because the direction of your life depends on who is in control. You must take an assessment and figure out first what you want to happen in your life. Do you want it to go as smoothly as possible, or do you want to reach your end goal in the most difficult way possible? Most would say they want to take the smoother path, but is that true? We say we want a smoother route, but do we do what it takes to be on it? Now granted, everything in life won't always be a blissful walk in the park, but if we allow God to lead and guide us through this life, it will make what we have to deal with easier. Many of us try to lead our own lives, relying on our

4

own understanding and strength, but Proverbs 3:5-6 reminds us to, *"Trust in the Lord with all thine heart: And lean not unto thine own understanding. In all thy ways acknowledge him, And he shall direct thy paths."* God desires to see his people blessed and prepares a way for us to get to our place. It's our job to seek him and get on the correct path. How do we do that? You must seek God through his word and prayer and allow him to guide you. We must trust God and him to direct our paths. Psalm 23:1 says, *"The Lord is my shepherd: I shall not want."* By definition, a shepherd tends to the sheep or guides in a particular direction. We are the sheep the Lord tends to and guides to the correct path. Just as a shepherd leads and protects their sheep from outside forces, so does God with us. In Psalm 23, David describes the Lord as his shepherd. A shepherd's job is to guide, protect, and provide for the sheep. Without a shepherd, sheep are vulnerable to predators, harsh weather, and getting lost. In the same way, without God's guidance, we are vulnerable to the challenges and distractions of life. But when we allow God to lead, He provides everything we need—peace, direction, and protection..

There may be times when we find ourselves in a great position in life, at the top of our game, things are going great for us, and we have everything we think we want and need. There may also be times when we hit a rough patch, and it seems like everything we don't want, is coming our way and hitting us all at once. If you would allow God to guide you and your decisions, you wouldn't feel that way. There wouldn't be feelings of discontentment. Your life wouldn't feel like a roller-coaster of highs and lows you have no control over. God wants us to seek him for guidance because only he can show us the best path. When we wake up to begin our day, whether in the morning or at night, we should always seek God's face first and ask him what he would have us do.

God deals with everyone differently, so don't expect him to minister to you the way he would someone else. We are all different, and God deals with us accordingly. Throughout the Bible, we see examples of individuals who allowed God to lead them. Take Moses for instance. When God called him to lead the Israelites out of Egypt, Moses felt unsure and inadequate. But God reassured him, saying, *"I will be with thee"* (Exodus 3:12). Moses' willingness to follow God's lead resulted in one of the most miraculous events in history-the parting of the Red Sea. Another example is Esther. When faced with the daunting task of saving her people from destruction, Esther relied on God's guidance. She fasted and prayed before approaching the king, and her obedience led to the deliverance of the Jewish people. You never know how your willingness to be led by God will affect your life or the lives of others.

The word of God tells us, *"For I know the thoughts that I think toward you, saith the Lord, thoughts of peace and not of evil, to give you an expected end."* (Jeremiah 29:11). If God knows the thoughts, he thinks towards us and wants to give us an expected end, shouldn't we be asking him for the advice for our lives instead of our friends who do not know what our expected end is? Yes, our friends may have the best intentions and believe they are giving us the advice we need, but God is the one who knows all and has all the answers that we need. The word goes on to say, *"Then shall ye call upon me, and ye shall go and pray unto me, and I will hearken unto you. And*

7

*ye shall seek me, and find me, when ye shall search for me with all your heart."* (Jeremiah 29:12-13) God wants us to call on him, to pray to him, to seek him, and in return, he will answer us. If we go to God, seeking him with all our heart, he will always answer us. We may not always get the answers we are looking for, but he will give us an answer that best suits the situation and His purpose for our lives. One thing you can be sure of is if you do not allow God to lead your life, you can make a pure mess of it on your own. Once you realize that only God can fix what you've made a mess of, God can come in, clean you up in the midst of your mess, and help you clean up the mess you created. The first mistake we make when we realize that we need God to fix things is thinking he will come in like a fairy Godmother, wave a magic wand, and make things all better. That is most certainly not the case. God will give us the tools to get back on track, but those tools are obtained in the time we spend seeking his face, praying, and fasting.

When all hell is breaking loose in our lives, most believers will run to the church leaders, seeking all of the help they can get, still not realizing that our help comes from the source, and the source is God. If we have leaders who hear from God, they can give instructions or a needed word through them, but we still have to get the fullness of those instructions and that word from God for ourselves. To obtain the things we desire while we are here on earth, *we must first seek the kingdom of God and his righteousness, then will all things be added unto us* (Matthew 6:33). What does that mean exactly? It means we must first seek the spiritual things of God. We must focus on doing Kingdom work, and then manifestations of our labor will come to fruition. All this comes from getting into a relationship with God and allowing him to lead and guide us through life. It's not about "religion" or the church's traditions but about your personal and intimate relationship with God. Some weapons and obstacles will still come against us, but can you imagine how much more inner peace we will have if we truly surrender our lives to God and allow him to lead us in every area? You won't have to wonder if your decisions are the best because you have already sought God, and he has given you the answers. You wouldn't have to worry if now is the time to start your business because he has already given you the "green light," as my Pastor would say. Your days of worrying would be gone, and you would be more confident in your decision-making because the Holy Spirit guides all your decisions. One of the biggest challenges in allowing God to lead is discerning His voice. In a world filled with noise-social media, opinions, and societal pressures-it can be difficult to hear God's still small voice. But Jesus assures us in John 10:27. *"My sheep hear my voice, and I know them, and they follow me."* To discern Gods voice we must spend time in his word and in prayer. The more we familiarize ourselves with his character and promises, the easier it becomes to recognize his guidance. Additionally, seeking godly counsel from trusted mentors or pastors can help confirm what God is speaking to you. Stop guessing at life, stop wondering what you should do, and stop asking friends and family for their opinions. I am not saying not to take wise counsel into account, but at the end of the day, the truest and unbiased answers you need come from God. God's answer is not an opinion but a fact because he and he alone know what is in store for you on the path ahead and will equip you accordingly. So, stop trying to lead your own life, stop allowing outside influences to dictate your decisions, but allow God to lead you to your Purpose. Take some time to self-reflect and ask yourself, who's leading you?

**Take a moment to reflect on the following questions:**

1.  Who or what is currently leading your life? Is it your own desires, societal expectations or God?

2.  Are there areas where you've been hesitant to surrender control to God? Why?

3.  What steps can you take to allow God to lead you more fully?

Use *The Path to Purpose: Reflection Guide* to write down your answers and pray over them. Ask God to reveal any areas where you need to surrender control and trust him more.

# CHAPTER 2

## ADJUST YOUR THINKING

"**Y**ou bring about what you think about." This is a quote I often hear my Apostle recite in his teachings. You are what you think; take a moment to think about that quote. What are you thinking about? This simple yet profound statement holds the key to transforming your life. Your thoughts have the power to shape your reality. Proverbs 23:7 says, *"For as he thinketh in his heart, so is he;"* In other words, your thoughts determine your actions, and your actions determine your outcomes. So we are what we think about, and what we think in our hearts becomes what we are. This was the topic of the lesson at Bible Study at my church one evening. Our Apostle broke this word down so simply that even children could understand. Everything we think about is our choice. We cannot blame the enemy for making us continually think about something. He can put a thought there, but we decide to either allow that thought to fester and magnify or reject it and replace it with a positive one. We must be intentional about what we are thinking about consciously and subconsciously.

What thoughts are we dwelling on throughout the day? What is our inner chatter saying? Are those thoughts conducive to productivity or spiritual growth? Are those thoughts being a hindrance and causing us to stay in the same place? Bringing your thoughts under subjection allows God to impart more spiritual blessings to you. It allows your mind to free up space for positive thoughts; if it is free of negative thinking, you can change what is drawn to you. Simply said, your internal thinking can influence your external outcome. Romans 12:2 instructs us to, *"be not conformed to this world, but be ye transformed by the renewing of your mind."* In order to walk in purpose, we must first renew our minds. This means replacing negative, self-defeating thoughts with positive, God-centered ones. It means shifting our focus from what we lack to to what God has already provided. One of the most powerful examples of a renewed mind is the transformation of Saul into Paul. Saul was a persecutor of Christians, but after encountering Jesus on the road to Damascus, his mind was renewed. He went from an enemy of the Gospel to one of its greatest advocates. This transformation was only possible because Saul allowed God to change his thinking. This is one of many examples that it is necessary to adjust your thinking and the way you think about and speak to yourself. To adjust your thinking and allow God to move in your life, you must first, wait for it, have an intimate relationship with him. Yes, this is a repeat of the earlier chapter, and it is because it is imperative to have a close relationship with God to obtain all that he has for us. The more intimate your relationship becomes with God, the more you are in tune with him, and he can reveal his secrets to you. This allows you to walk in the power and authority that has already been given to you. I'm sure we can agree that most people would like to know everything they can about their spouse or potential spouse. They want to be as close as they can be and know every intimate detail to know how to please their other half or not upset them. God wants the same kind of relationship. Just like we want to please our spouses, we should desire to please God.

God wants us to know him, just like we want to know others, but more! This comes by way of changing your mindset and not seeing God as someone to pray to in your time of trouble, but to talk with him all the time. We will always need God, so to minimize the time you call on him to only when you're in trouble or dire need is an insult to the Father and yourself. You are robbing yourself of getting to truly know the one who knows everything about you and still loves and cares for you. Taking the necessary time daily to nurture our relationship with God will open our eyes and understanding to many things they were closed to. We would better understand God's inner workings and how to live our lives capitalizing on our unlimited potential. You must become very intentional when changing your thinking and lifestyle. For me, it was making a schedule for myself. I look at things as "if I can schedule it, I can do it." Don't get me wrong: it was and sometimes still is a struggle because I am making myself do things outside my normal routine. I have learned that I won't get the desired results if I don't do this. I know I must set my intimate time with God before my kids get up and we start our day, or I will never get to it. I also take time out to encourage myself because if we are to be honest, there will be times when no one will be available to encourage you. When you take the time to encourage yourself and remind yourself that *you can do all things through Christ who strengthens you* (Philippians 4:13), you gain more strength and also deepen your connection with God through his word. When it comes to controlling the thoughts you have, my Apostle gave us some great advice on what he does. Whenever the enemy tries to put a thought in his mind, he shuts it down right then and lets him know that it isn't his thought, and he can take it back to where he got it from and send it back to the dry places, it has no power in him. That is so powerful! Many people think they must accept their thoughts because they don't understand they can reject them. You have the power to reject them, my friends! Reject those negative thoughts. The enemy has no power over your mind; he can't control it; he can only do what **YOU** allow him to do! But let's be clear: it is not just the negative thoughts we have to take control of; it is all of our thoughts and inner chatter. Negative thoughts can be like weeds in a garden-if left unchecked, they can choke out the good things God is trying to grow in your life. But just as a gardener pulls weeds, you can uproot negative thoughts and replace them with God's truth. For example, if you find yourself thinking, *"I'm not good enough,"* replace that thought with, *I am fearfully and wonderfully made"(Psalm 139:4)* If you are struggling with fear, remind yourself, *"God has not given you the spirit of fear, but of power, and of love, and of a sound mind."(2 Timothy 1:7)*. There are plenty of references in the word of God that can help you to overcome fears and negative self-talk.

**Practical Strategies for Adjusting Your Thinking**

- **Daily Affirmtions:** Start each day by speaking God's promises over your life. For example, *"I am loved by God,"* I am capable of achieving my goals," or "God has a plan for my life."*

- **Gratitude Journal:** Write down three things you're grateful for each day. Gratitude shifts your focus from what's wrong to what's right.

- **Meditate on Scripture:** Spend time meditating on Bible verses that speak to your situation. Write them down and reflect on them throughout the day.

   In Psalm 23, David describes the Lord as his shepherd. A shepherd's job is to guide, protect, and provide for the sheep. Without a shepherd, sheep are vulnerable to predators, harsh weather, and getting lost. In the same way, without God's guidance, we are vulnerable to the challenges and distractions of life. But when we allow God to lead, He provides everything we need—peace, direction, and protection.We could have thoughts that would be seemingly innocent and would not hurt anyone, but ask yourself, is it a thought that God would approve of? If not, reject it and replace it with something positive and productive. There are a lot of things that we are missing because we have not adjusted our thinking completely. Maybe we no longer speak negatively about others, but what are we saying about ourselves? That is the one right there. What are you saying to yourself about yourself when you are not around your friends, associates, or coworkers? Are you uplifting yourself, looking at the things you have not accomplished yet or where you could have been? Are you looking at what you used to do or how you cannot get your head above water? If these are some of your thoughts, my friends, you will never reach your full Purpose and potential thinking this way. Unless you adjust those thoughts, you will always be where you are.

Everything we go through is a learning lesson, whether it be things we cause ourselves or things God allowed for us to grow. Either way, for those who love God, he is working our situations out for our good (Romans 8:28); what we need to do is not fight against what God wants to do in our lives. We can help God help us by changing our way of thinking. Stop thinking negatively about yourself and your situation, and start thinking about how to change amid your circumstances. Look for the rainbow that comes after the storm. No matter what your storm looks like, how dark and cloudy it is, or how long it may last, you know a light is waiting to shine through the darkness. Do your best not to dwell on what you see or don't see because your life will always reflect that; instead, focus on replacing negative thoughts with positive ones. What do you want to accomplish? When you see the storm, think of the beautiful clear blue skies you saw the day before and will see again once the storm clears. You can use many different strategies to adjust your thinking; you just have to be willing to commit to using them. You must want more for yourself and be willing to see yourself living beyond mediocrity, living a life you thought was only in your dreams. You must know there *is* more for you, that God *has* more for you. Let what you become to be a product of your thinking. Let your thinking be a product of your time with God. Let your time with God help shape how you view yourself, others, and life. To do any of this, you must be willing to Adjust your Thinking.

**Practical Exercises to Renewing your mind:**

- Identify a negative thought pattern that's been holding you back.
- Find a Bible verse that counters that thought.

Write the verse down and commit to meditating on it daily.

# CHAPTER 3

## WRITE THE VISION

**H**ave you ever attended an event with an itinerary of exactly how the day was to progress? These events can include a wedding, a church function, a conference, or something to that effect. Every detail was written out either on an itinerary or on the program. You knew what was happening, where to be, and when to be there. You knew how long each session would last, when you would break for lunch, and when the event would end. This is one example of writing the vision and making it plain. When it was all over, I am sure the visionary and coordinator of the event breathed a sigh of relief that the event was over, their vision came to pass, and everything went according to plan. But what happens when things don't go according to plan? Do we give up, or do we go back to the drawing board? Society has taken the scripture "write the vision and make it plain" and run with it, which isn't bad. The problem arises when it is the only part of the scripture focused on and not what goes beyond it. If you read Habakkuk 2:2-3, it reads, *"And the Lord answered me, and said, Write the vision, and make it plain upon tables, that he may run that readeth it. For the vision is yet for an appointed time, but at the end, it shall speak, and not lie; though it tarry, wait for it: because it will surely come, it will not tarry."* Writing the vision comes with not only writing down what you desire to do, but also making a plan of action. How else can you be successful with your dream unless you plan for it?

Habakkuk 2:2 is a call to action scripture. Writing down your vision is more than just a motivational exercise; it is a spiritual practice that aligns your heart with God's plan for your life. Without a clear vision, it's easy to get off track. Proverbs 29:18(a) says, *"Where there is no vision, the people perish."* When we lack direction, we become susceptible to distractions and detours. But when we have a clear vision, we can stay focused on what truly matters. Although plans may need to be adjusted or changed, you are still working on the plan. No matter how bumpy the road may get, choose to stay on the course because, in your staying and sowing, you will reap the harvest you never knew you could have. Remember that when you write your vision, you must also mix in prayer and add fasting for some real power and results.

A popular trend is "Vision Boards"; some people even get together and have vision board parties where they gather together with poster boards, magazine cutouts, and more to create a visual interpretation of things they desire for their lives. Digital vision boards are also being created, which can be kept on devices or printed out and framed. Whichever route you choose in "writing out your vision," there are some things to remember. While writing out the vision and creating something to keep before you, prayer and belief must also be incorporated to keep said vision alive.

## Creating Your Vision Board

A vision board is a powerful tool for visualizing your goals and dreams. It is a physical representation of what you want to achieve, and it serves as a daily reminder of where you are headed. Here is how you can create your own.

- **Gather Materials:** You will need a poster board, magazines, glue, scisscors, and markers. If creating a digital board, you can use **Canva**(free & paid options)
- **Choose Images and Words:** Arrange the images and words on the board in a way that inspires you. Then, glue them down.
- **Arrange and Glue:** Arrange the images and words on the board in a way that inspires you. Then, glue them down.
- **Display Your Board:** Place your vision board somewhere you'll see it every day, like your bedroom or office.

There is a time when you will have to put in the work of praying to bring your vision to fruition. It is not going to create itself. Writing the vision for your life also means you need a connection to God. The closer the connection, the clearer the vision becomes. The quieter your inner chatter is, the easier for God to speak to you. The more you work on your inner being, the more it is reflected on the outer. God can easily speak and direct instructions to you when you silence the noise in your mind and around you and give yourself completely to him. It comes back to having that intimate relationship with God. You have to be connected to him to truly hear and write out the vision for your life. What you see may be great, but it is greater when you tap into what God sees for you! When God reveals things to us or has us write down our visions, it is for a reason and a purpose. If we open our eyes to see, we are watching a written vision unfold today. Just read Revelations.

In Revelation 2:19, Jesus told John to *"write the things which thou hast seen and the things which are, and the things which shall be hereafter."* The book of Revelation is an entire vision given to John, and he wrote it down as instructed for all who would receive it, warning us of what was to come and giving us a glimpse of what we will see in Heaven. These visions not only served as a guide for the early church but also a source of hope and encouragement for believers through the ages. Another example is

Nehemiah. When he heard about the broken walls of Jerusalem, he felt called to rebuild them. But before he took action, he spent time in prayer and fasting, seeking God's guidance. Then, he created a detailed plan and rallied the people to work together. Because Nehemiah had a clear vision, he was able to accomplish what seemed impossible.

Isaiah 8:1 says, "Moreover the Lord said unto me, take thee a great roll, and write in it with a man's pen concerning Mahershalahashbaz." this was a specific detail and instruction God gave Isaiah to do. At that time Isaiah was a great prophet and had predicted the fall of Israel and Syria. God had him write and display that vision so everyone could see, read, and heed the warning. Just as God used Isaiah then, he can use you just the same, if not more. You never know how your vision for your life could impact you and your family and others.

There is great significance in writing out the vision. It puts it before you and serves as a reminder, but it is also for you to read daily, not just glance at it as you're walking by, but read, acknowledge, and meditate on what is before you. Seeing it in your mind and seeing it brought into reality. The word of God, the Bible, is an entire written vision from Genesis to Revelation. The authors of each book were Holy Spirit inspired and wrote the vision to be used for God's people, past, present, and future. Writing the vision and making it plain is not just for our benefit, to improve our lives; it's also to sound the alarm and let the people know what is to come and lead people to the one true and living God, not leading them to ourselves. We are God's children, his servants, his disciples. We have a duty to perform and need to be always connected to God to perform it. You, I, all of us, have been given instructions to write the vision, just make sure you are in position and connected to receive the vision. Get and stay connected to God, follow the instructions set forth by him, and be in a position to hear the vision so that you may Write the Vision.

**Practical Exercise: Writing Your Vision**

- Take out a notebook or journal.

- Write down your vision for the next year, five years, and ten years.

- Include specific goals, such as career aspirations, personal growth, and spiritual development.

- Pray over vision and ask God to guide you as you work toward it.

# CHAPTER 4

## WORKING YOUR FAITH

───◦⟋⟍◦───

**H**ave you been believing in God for something that hasn't happened yet? Have you put your petitions before him? Have you started taking the necessary steps to get where you desire to be? If you haven't, the good news is you have time to get started on it! The word tells us, *"Even so faith, if it hath not works, is dead, being alone." "For as the body without the spirit is dead, so faith without works is dead also"* (James 2:17;26). This powerful statement reminds us that faith is not just about believing-it is about taking action. If you want to see your dreams come to fruition, you must be willing to put in the work. Many people misunderstand faith as passive trust, waiting for God to do everything, but biblical faith is active. It requires us to step out, even when we don't see the full picture.

Faith without action is like expecting a harvest without planting seeds. Imagine a farmer praying for a bountiful crop but never tiling the soil, planting seeds, or watering the ground. No matter how much faith he has, without action, no harvest will come. Likewise, God expects us to trust him while actively preparing for the blessings He has in store. Hebrews 11:1 defines faith as: *"Now faith is the substance of things hoped for, the evidence of things not seen."* This means that faith requires us to move forward even when we do not see immediate results.

Abraham is often referred to as the father of faith. When God promised him a son, Abraham believed, even though he and his wife, Sarah, were well past childbearing age. But Abraham did not just sit back and wait-he took steps to prepare for the promise. He and Sarah moved to a new land, and they remained faithful to God's plan even when it seemed impossible. Because of his faith and actions, Abraham became the father of many nations. God will bless your efforts, but you must PUT IN THE EFFORT! Yes, God also can make anything happen for us because there are no limitations to what he can do.

Faith and action go hand in hand. Think about it this way: if you believe God has called you to start a business, you cannot just sit back and wait for it to happen. You need to take steps like creating a business plan, networking, and seeking mentor-ship. Your faith fuels your actions, and your actions demonstrate your faith. Your Faith can be bigger than anyone could ever imagine and you could have huge dreams of a better life, but if you are not taking the necessary steps to get there, you will never attain what you dream about. One of the greatest demonstrations of faith in action is found in Matthew 14:28-31 when Peter walked on water:

*"And Peter answered him and said, Lord, if it be thou, bid me come unto thee on the water. And he said, Come. And when Peter was come down out of the ship, he walked on the water, to go to Jesus."*

Peter experienced the miraculous because he was willing to step out of the boat. However, the moment he allowed fear to distract him, he began to sink. This teaches us that our faith must remain focused on Christ. The moment we shift our eyes to our circumstances rather than God's promises, doubt creeps in.

## Overcoming Barriers to Active Faith

- **Fear of Failure** – Many hesitate to step out in faith because they fear failing. But remember, even if Peter sank, Jesus was right there to catch him.

- **Waiting for the "Perfect" Time** – There is no perfect moment to start. Ecclesiastes 11:4 says, *"He that observeth the wind shall not sow; and he that regardeth the clouds shall not reap."* Take the step now.

- **Listening to Doubters** – Surround yourself with faith-filled individuals who will encourage, not discourage, your walk.

- **Lack of Patience** – God's promises come in His timing. Keep moving forward, even when progress seems slow.

Faith needs belief and action. Think about it this way. If you want to lose weight, you will not continue to sit on the couch and do nothing, right? You might begin with a smaller routine by walking, then jogging, then progress into a full-blown run and incorporating changes to your diet. Eventually you lose the weight you want and will reach your goal if you stay consistent. On the contrary, if you decide to just sit there and believe the weight will fall off on its own accord, then my friend, you will still be sitting at the same weight you started with if not more pounds added. The same can be said for whatever goal you have set before you. Yes, you may have the Faith to believe it will happen, but if you are not taking the necessary steps to bring it forth, you just have a dream written on paper.

My question for you to ponder on is, would you appreciate it if he just dropped what you wanted into your lap? Be honest with yourself and really think about this question. Here's the thing, and I'm going to be quite candid here, some of us are just so lazy! Some of us have things we desire or need from God, but we want him to give us the completed solution, not the instructions and ingredients to complete it ourselves. For example, I strongly desire a strawberry cheesecake, one of my favorite cakes, so I ask God for it because I know he gives me the desires of my heart. Well, he gives me the cheesecake, in the form of the ingredients for me to make myself. I'm looking at it and saying to myself, well, Lord, I asked for a cheesecake, but I wanted it already made, even though I am well capable of following instructions and could make it myself. Although this is a scenario, I already know the answer God would give me if I asked him. I could hear him clearly saying: if I just gave it to you, your appreciation would be there, but not as much as when you took the ingredients, I gave you and created it yourself. God wants to give us the things we desire, but he wants us to also put our hands on the plow and work toward it.

### Practical Steps for Working Your Faith

- **Set Goals:** Break your vision down into smaller, actionable goals. For example, if your vision is to write a book, set a goal to write 500 words a day.

- **Pray and Seek Guidance** – Faith is not reckless ambition; it is divine alignment. Seek God's wisdom before taking action (Proverbs 3:5-6).

- **Step Out in Obedience** – Even if you don't have all the answers, start moving in the direction God has called you.

- **Daily Declarations:** Speak God's promises over your life. Say, *"I walk by faith, not by sight"* (2 Corinthians 5:7).

- **Faith Journal:** Record moments where God has come through for you to remind yourself of His faithfulness.

- **Take One Step Daily:** Start working on your goals, even if it is just a small step. Remember, progress is progress, no matter how small. Even small steps of obedience build momentum.

- **Stay Consistent:** Consistency is key. Even when you do not feel motivated, keep taking steps toward your vision. Faith requires perseverance.

Just as a seed takes time to grow, results come from sustained effort.

- **Surround Yourself with Encouragement** – Build relationships with people who will challenge you to keep believing and taking action.

Just as God has created all life on earth and us in his image, he wants us to do the same and create! God shaped and molded us with his hands. Are we greater than God that we can't get down and create the life we want with our hands and his help guiding us? When you have a dream, you desire to bring to fruition, how great would it make you feel knowing that your hands worked it, that you did not sit idly hoping that it would happen, but you got up, exercised your Faith, worked toward your vision and God blessed your efforts? I know that would be a feeling of pure joy for myself. Think about it this way: it is like raising a baby; you feed it, clean it, nurture it, and have the Faith to believe that everything will work out as it should while still doing all you can to raise your baby to be all it can be. Your vision is your baby, your

Purpose is your baby, and while you have the Faith to believe that it will happen, you still work to make it grow, and God does what he does to make it prosper. Having Faith is always a remarkable thing to have, no matter how small or how large. In having that Faith, you still need to have a work ethic, believing in God for the things you cannot do on your own and working on the things you can. You are meant to be successful, just don't get caught up in having Faith alone, get busy doing the work. Work your Faith, and your Faith will work for you!

### Practical Exercise: Faith in Action

- Identify one area of your life where you need to exercise more faith.

- Write down one action step you can take today to move closer to your goal.

- Pray for God's guidance, strength and courage to keep walking even when the outcome isn't immediate.

Faith is about movement, about trusting God enough to act. As you work your faith, you will find that God meets you at every step, guiding, strengthening, and providing for your journey.

# CHAPTER 5

## OVERCOMING OBSTACLES

**N**o journey is not without its challenges. When you are walking in your purpose you can expect to face obstacles along the way. But the good news is that God has already given you everything you need to overcome them. Obstacles are not meant to destroy you; they are meant to develop you. They strengthen your faith, build resilience, and prepare your for the greater things God has in store.

Obstacles test our faith and commitment to our purpose. When we face challenges, it often feels as though we are being pulled in multiple directions, and the weight of those challenges can feel unbearable at times. Yet, as James 1:2-4 reminds us: *"My brethren, count it all joy when ye fall into divers temptations; Knowing this, that the trying of your faith worketh patience. But let patience have her perfect work, that ye may be perfect and entire, wanting nothing."* This scripture is a powerful reminder that our trials are not setbacks; they are divine tools for refining us. They are designed to develop our faith, patience, and ultimately bring us closer to the person God has called us to be.

In my own life, I've faced many obstacles that have tested my faith and commitment to my purpose. There were times when I felt uncertain, overwhelmed, and discouraged. But looking back, I can see how each of those challenges shaped me, strengthened my resolve, and sharpened my understanding of my purpose. One significant example was when I first decided to step into the world of self-publishing. The process seemed daunting, filled with unknowns, and I faced many setbacks—technical difficulties, financial constraints, and even moments of self-doubt. There were days when I questioned whether I was on the right path, but God reminded me to trust in His timing and to remain faithful to the vision He had placed in my heart.

Instead of viewing these obstacles as barriers, I began to see them as opportunities for growth. I realized that each challenge I faced was a chance for me to build resilience, strengthen my trust in God, and develop the skills necessary to succeed. Through each struggle, I learned valuable lessons about perseverance and the importance of staying connected to God's guidance. I also discovered the power of patience—something that didn't come naturally to me, but through my trials, I was able to develop. Patience is not simply waiting—it is an active trust in God's plan, even when you can't see the outcome.

For instance, when I was working on my book *Dear Woman of God*, the writing process was far from smooth. There were moments of frustration, where the words wouldn't flow, and times when I felt like giving up altogether. But each time I faced a creative block, I reminded myself that this obstacle was refining my craft. It taught me to trust in the process, to lean on my faith, and to embrace the times when things didn't go according to plan. Those moments were not wasted. They were moments of growth that helped me become a better writer, a better communicator, and a stronger woman of faith.

I can also reflect on the challenges I faced with my brand, *Sufficiently Covered*. There were times when I wondered if the vision was too big, or if I was capable of handling the responsibilities that came with it. It wasn't easy to step into a space that was unfamiliar, especially as I balanced multiple roles and personal commitments. But each obstacle that arose—from figuring out how to manage the business side of things to creating content for the programs I wanted to offer—pushed me to learn and grow. There were times I doubted myself, but those moments taught me to trust God more deeply, lean into my faith, and accept that growth sometimes comes through struggle.

Through these experiences, I have learned that obstacles are not just obstacles; they are opportunities for refinement. Just like gold is refined in fire, our faith, character, and purpose are refined through the challenges we face. God allows us to go through difficulties not to break us but to mold us into the individuals we are meant to be. Every difficulty is a part of the process that God uses to develop our patience, perseverance, and ultimately our purpose.

When we encounter obstacles, our initial reaction may be to question God or feel as if we are being punished. However, we must remember that God doesn't send trials to hurt us—He sends them to help us grow. The trying of our faith produces patience, and as the scripture in James encourages us, we are to let patience have its perfect work. This process may not be easy, but it is necessary.

For example, as a writer, I've faced numerous obstacles in my journey. I've dealt with self-doubt, critical feedback, and moments where I thought my writing would never reach the people it was meant to touch. In these moments, my faith was tested. But through each negative encounter, I learned to rely on God more deeply. I learned that His timing is perfect, and that even in the silence, He is at work behind the scenes. Those moments of rejection and doubt became the very soil in which my perseverance and trust grew.

Similarly, when it comes to walking in purpose, there will be obstacles that seem to arise just when you are on the verge of success. Perhaps it's a financial setback, a relationship strain, or an unexpected health issue. These challenges may feel like stumbling blocks, but they are, in reality, stepping stones to greater spiritual maturity. Each trial pushes you to lean into God's strength and trust in His provision. They are opportunities for you to deepen your faith and commit even more fully to your purpose, no matter how difficult it may seem.

It's crucial to remember that God's purpose for your life will always be greater than any obstacle you face. When you encounter difficulties, ask yourself: *How is God using this challenge to refine me?* Whether it's building patience, teaching you to rely on His strength, or giving you the tools to become more resilient, every obstacle serves a purpose in your spiritual growth.

Obstacles force us to grow in ways we wouldn't have if everything had gone smoothly. If everything in life were easy, we wouldn't learn the depth of God's faithfulness, His ability to provide in times of need, and His power to turn our struggles into triumphs. When we come out of the fire, we are not just refined—we are stronger, wiser, and more aligned with God's will for our lives.

I encourage you to view obstacles through a new lens. Instead of seeing them as roadblocks, view them as opportunities to grow, trust God more, and move closer to fulfilling your purpose. Every challenge, no matter how difficult, is a chance to see God's faithfulness in action and to become more of the person He has called you to be.

As you continue on your journey, remember that your faith will always be tested. But each test is an opportunity to grow and become the person God has created you to be. Embrace the trials, knowing that they are not just obstacles—they are the stepping stones that will lead you to your purpose. Trust that God is with you every step of the way, and that with every obstacle you overcome, you are becoming more like the person He has designed you to be.

# Common Obstacles to Purpose and How to Overcome Them

- **Fear and Doubt** – One of the greatest obstacles is self-doubt and fear of failure. Fear can cripple us and keep us from stepping into our calling. The Bible reminds us in 2 Timothy 1:7: *"For God hath not given us the spirit of fear; but of power, and of love, and of a sound mind."*

  - ❖ Overcome fear by reminding yourself of God's promises.

  - ❖ Take small, actionable steps in faith, even when fear tries to paralyze you.

- **Lack of Resources** – Sometimes, we feel like we don't have enough—money, connections, knowledge—to fulfill our purpose. But Philippians 4:19 assures us: *"But my God shall supply all your need according to his riches in glory by Christ Jesus."*

❖ Trust that God will provide what you need in His timing.

❖ Be resourceful and seek opportunities where God has already placed you.

● **Naysayers and Negative Influences** – Not everyone will understand or support your vision. Some people may doubt you, discourage you, or even oppose you.

❖ Surround yourself with a community that uplifts and encourages you (Proverbs 27:17).

❖ Do not allow others' doubts to dictate your steps—seek God's affirmation above all else.

● **Delays and Waiting Seasons** – Sometimes, things don't happen as quickly as we expect. We can feel stuck, wondering if we are on the right path.

❖ Remember that waiting is not wasted time. God is preparing you for the next level (Isaiah 40:31).

❖ Use waiting seasons to grow spiritually, sharpen your skills, and strengthen your faith.

● **Personal Weaknesses and Limitations** – We often feel unqualified or inadequate for the calling God has placed on our lives.

❖ God specializes in using the weak to accomplish great things (2 Corinthians 12:9-10).

❖ Instead of focusing on what you lack, lean on God's strength and allow Him to work through you.

Joseph's life was filled with seemingly insurmountable obstacles—betrayal by his own brothers, false accusations, and unjust imprisonment. Yet, despite facing these challenges, Joseph remained steadfast in his faith and commitment to God's purpose for his life. His journey is a powerful reminder that no matter how difficult the obstacles may seem, God is always working behind the scenes to position us for greater things.

Joseph's story began with his brothers' jealousy. They were so consumed with hatred that they sold him into slavery, leaving him abandoned and betrayed. I can only imagine the hurt and confusion Joseph must have felt. How could his own flesh and blood turn against him in such a way? For many of us, betrayal is one of the hardest obstacles to overcome, especially when it comes from those we love and trust. In moments like these, it's easy to question God's plan and wonder why we are facing such pain. Yet Joseph's story teaches us that even in the midst of betrayal, God has a greater purpose at work.

Joseph didn't let his circumstances define him. When he was sold into Potiphar's house, he rose to prominence because of his integrity and his trust in God. But even in this seemingly favorable situation, another obstacle arose—Potiphar's wife falsely accused him of a crime he didn't commit, and Joseph was thrown into prison. Again, his circumstances seemed unfair, and his dreams must have felt far away. How many times have we faced what feels like an inexplicable setback? How often do we feel that the injustice of the world is too much to bear? Yet, just like Joseph, we are called to remain faithful, even when the path ahead doesn't make sense. Joseph's response to these obstacles was not bitterness or defeat; it was trust in God's purpose.

While Joseph was in prison, he continued to demonstrate faithfulness and excellence. He interpreted dreams for fellow prisoners, knowing that this was the gift God had given him. And in God's perfect timing, Joseph's gift of interpretation was brought to the attention of Pharaoh, leading to his rise as a leader in Egypt. He went from being a prisoner to becoming the second-in-command of an entire nation. What a remarkable transformation! This turnaround wasn't a result of Joseph's own doing—it was God working through Joseph's obedience and faithfulness in the midst of adversity.

Joseph's story culminates in one of the most profound moments of forgiveness and redemption in Scripture. After years of hardship, Joseph's brothers came to Egypt seeking food during a famine. When they didn't recognize him, Joseph had the opportunity to seek revenge, but instead, he chose to forgive them and help them. He understood that God had allowed everything to happen to position him to save lives, including their lives, during the famine. This is a powerful testimony of God's ability to turn our obstacles into opportunities for growth and reconciliation.

Joseph's statement in Genesis 50:20 reflects this deep understanding of God's sovereignty: *"But as for you, ye thought evil against me; but God meant it unto good, to bring to pass, as it is this day, to save much people alive."* Joseph was able to see the bigger picture of God's plan. What others meant for harm, God used for good. What appeared to be a series of unfortunate events was actually a divine orchestration that led Joseph to fulfill his purpose. His life became a testimony of how God can take the most difficult circumstances and turn them into a platform for His glory.

In my own life, I've experienced moments when I couldn't understand why certain obstacles were placed in my path. There were times when I felt as though I had been betrayed or overlooked, and I questioned whether I was truly following the right path. But as I look back, I can see that each obstacle was not in my life by accident. Each trial, each setback, was a stepping stone that brought me closer to where I am now. Just like Joseph, there were times when it felt as though my dreams were far out of reach, but God used those very moments to refine my character, deepen my faith, and equip me for the work He had called me to do.

There was a particular instance in my journey where I was faced with a major setback in a project I was working on. Everything seemed to fall apart all at once—the funding fell through, the timing seemed off, and I found myself questioning whether I was really meant to pursue this endeavor. In those moments, I reminded myself of Joseph's story. I chose to hold onto the truth that even in the midst of obstacles, God had a greater plan. Instead of giving up, I sought God's direction, and as I continued to move forward in faith, things began to fall into place in ways that I couldn't have orchestrated myself. God used that setback to position me for something bigger than I had originally envisioned.

## The Power of Faith and Obedience

Joseph's life reminds us that faith and obedience in the face of adversity are key to fulfilling God's purpose for our lives. When we remain faithful and trust in God's timing, even in the most difficult circumstances, we are positioning ourselves for breakthroughs that will impact not just our own lives but the lives of others. Joseph's obedience saved not only his family but an entire nation, and through his story, we can see that our obedience to God can have a ripple effect that reaches far beyond what we can imagine.

As we walk through life, we will undoubtedly face challenges—betrayal, disappointment, and unfair treatment. However, Joseph's life teaches us that obstacles are not the end of the story. They are opportunities for God to reveal His power, to refine our faith, and to position us for greater things. Like Joseph, we may not understand the purpose of our trials in the moment, but we can trust that God is working all things together for our good. Just as He used Joseph's faithfulness to bring about a greater good, He will use our obstacles to fulfill His purpose in our lives.

So, when you face challenges, remember Joseph. Instead of viewing them as insurmountable barriers, see them as opportunities for growth and refinement. God can turn what was meant for harm into a platform for His glory. Just as Joseph saved many lives during a time of famine, your faithfulness in adversity may be the key to unlocking something greater in your life and the lives of those around you.

## Practical Strategies for Overcoming Obstacles

- **Prayer and Fasting:** When faced with a challenge, seek God through prayer and fasting. Ask Him for wisdom and strength.

- **Stay Focused:** Keep your eyes on your vision, even when the road gets tough. Remember why you started and where you're headed.
- **Seek Support:** Don't be afraid to ask for help. Surround yourself with people who will encourage and support you.
- **Learn from Failure:** Every obstacle is an opportunity to learn and grow. Don't let failure discourage you—use it as a stepping stone to success.

**Practical Exercise: Facing Your Obstacles**

- Identify one obstacle you're currently facing.
- Write down one action step you can take to overcome it.
- Pray for God's guidance and strength as you face this challenge.
- Find a scripture that speaks to your situation and meditate on it daily.

Remember, obstacles are not signs that you should give up. They are indicators that you are moving in the right direction. Press forward, knowing that with

God, you have the power to overcome anything standing in your way.

# CHAPTER 6

## LIVING A LIFE OF GRATITUDE

G ratitude is a powerful tool for shifting your perspective and staying focused on your purpose. When you cultivate a heart of gratitude, you begin to see God's hand in every area of your life. Gratitude is not just a fleeting emotion but a posture of the heart that allows us to recognize and appreciate God's presence in both the extraordinary and the ordinary moments of life It is more than just saying "thank you"- it is a transformative mindset that shifts our focus from what we lack to the abundant blessings already present in our lives. When we cultivate heart of gratitude, we acknowledge God's goodness in all circumstances, even in challenges.

Have you ever gone through a difficult season, only to look back later and realize how much God was working behind the scenes? Gratitude allows us to acknowledge His faithfulness, even when we do not immediately see the outcome we desire. It reminds us that He is always at work, orchestrating events for our good.

Gratitude has the power to change our perspective. Instead of dwelling on setbacks, we begin to see them as setups for greater things.When we cultivate a heart of gratitude, we acknowledge God's goodness in all circumstances, even in challenges. Paul's life is a powerful example of this. He endured hardships, imprisonments, and persecution, yet he continuously praised God. In Philippians 4:6-7, Paul encourages us: *"Be careful for nothing; but in every thing by prayer and supplication with thanksgiving let your requests be made known unto God. And the peace of God, which passeth all understanding, shall keep your hearts and minds through Christ Jesus."*

Gratitude strengthens our faith, giving us peace that surpasses understanding. When we thank God, even before seeing the results, we demonstrate trust in His perfect plan. This is an act of faith—choosing to believe in God's goodness regardless of our circumstances.I remember a time when I was waiting for a breakthrough. Doors seemed to be closing, and discouragement was creeping in. One day, I decided to shift my focus. Instead of fixating on what hadn't happened, I started thanking God for everything He had already done. I thanked Him for the strength to keep going, for the lessons I was learning, and for His provision in ways I hadn't considered. That change in perspective didn't immediately change my situation, but it changed me. It deepened my trust in God and opened my eyes to blessings I had overlooked.

A heart of gratitude also shifts our focus from comparison to contentment. So often, we look at what others have, measuring our success against their accomplishments. Social media has made it easier than ever to compare our lives to carefully curated highlights of others. However, when we practice gratitude, we recognize that God's timing and provision are unique for each of us. What He has for us is specifically designed for our journey.

Comparison robs us of joy, but gratitude restores our peace and reminds us that what God has for us is for us. Instead of asking, "Why don't I have what they have?" we begin asking, "Lord, how can I steward what You have given me?" This shift leads to greater contentment and joy.

## Developing a Gratitude Habit

- **Daily Reflections:** Start or end your day by listing five things you're grateful for. Keep a journal to reflect on how your gratitude grows over time.

- **Gratitude in Prayer:** Before asking God for anything, thank Him for what He has already done.

- **Expressing Appreciation:** Make it a habit to tell others you appreciate them. A simple note or kind word can uplift someone's spirit.

- **Gratitude in Challenges:** Ask yourself, "What is God teaching me in this season?" Even trials can be blessings in disguise.

- **Praise Through Worship:** Gratitude is expressed not just in words but in worship. Singing praises to God shifts our focus to His goodness and reminds us of His faithfulness.

In Luke 17, Jesus healed ten lepers, but only one returned to thank Him. Jesus asked, *"Were there not ten cleansed? But where are the nine?"* (Luke 17:17). This story reminds us of the importance of gratitude and that it is a choice. When we take the time to thank God for His blessings, we open the door for more blessings to flow into our lives. Are we among the nine who take blessings for granted, or are we the one who returns to give thanks?

Jesus told the one leper who returned *"Arise, go thy way: they faith hath made thee whole."* While all ten were healed, only the one who expressed gratitude was made whole. This teaches us that gratitude not only acknowledges what God has done but also positions us for a deeper transformation.

### Practical Ways to Cultivate Gratitude

- **Gratitude Journal:** Write down three things you're grateful for each day.
- **Thankful Prayers:** Start your prayers by thanking God for His blessings.
- **Acts of Kindness:** Show gratitude by serving others and giving back.

A grateful heart strengthens faith. When we intentionally focus on what God has already done, it increases our confidence in what He will do. David's life is a prime example. Before he faced Goliath, he recalled how God had delivered him from the lion and the bear (1 Samuel 17:37). His gratitude for past victories fueled his faith for future challenges. David didn't step onto the battlefield with uncertainty; he stepped forward with boldness because he had seen God's faithfulness before. His gratitude was not just a reflection on the past but a declaration of trust in God's future provision. When we remind ourselves of past victories, we strengthen our ability to trust God for future challenges. This is why it is important to keep a record of answered prayers and testimonies. Writing down what God has done allows us to revisit those moments when doubt tries to creep in.

Gratitude also cultivates joy. Proverbs 17:22 tells us, *"A merry heart doeth good like a medicine: but a broken spirit drieth the bones."* When we practice gratitude, we shift our mindset from worry to worship, from despair to joy. Have you ever noticed how difficult it is to feel anxious and grateful at the same time? When we choose gratitude, we replace fear with faith, negativity with hope, and stress with peace.

Gratitude is easy when life is going well, but what about when we face trials? Paul, who endured imprisonment, persecution, and hardship, still wrote in 1 Thessalonians 5:18: *"In every thing give thanks: for this is the will of God in Christ Jesus concerning you."* Paul wasn't saying to give thanks *for* all things, but rather to give thanks *in* all things. There is a difference. We may not be grateful for hardships, but we can be grateful for God's presence in the midst of them. We can thank Him for the strength He provides, the lessons we learn, and the growth we experience through challenges.

Here are some ways to remain grateful in tough times:

❖ **Look for Small Blessings:** Even in hardship, there is always something to be thankful for. Seek out moments of joy.

❖ **Remember Past Victories:** Reflect on times when God brought you through difficult seasons before.

❖ **Surround Yourself with Positive Influences:** Being around thankful people helps maintain a heart of gratitude.

❖ **Keep a Gratitude Jar:** Write down blessings as they come and read them when you need encouragement.

❖ **Pray for Strength:** Ask God to help you see the good in every situation, even when it is not immediately obvious.

**Practical Exercise: Gratitude Challenge**

● For the next seven days, write down three things you're grateful for each day.
● At the end of the week, reflect on how this practice has impacted your perspective.

# CHAPTER 7

## THE POWER OF COMMUNITY

Walking in purpose is not a solo journey. God created us to live in relationship with others, to encourage, uplift, and hold one another accountable. We were never meant to navigate life's challenges alone. From the very beginning, in Genesis 2:18, God declared, *"It is not good that the man should be alone."* While this verse is often associated with marriage, it also speaks to the broader truth that we are designed for connection. Community is essential for growth, healing, and fulfilling God's calling on our lives.

Think about the times in your life when you have faced hardships or uncertainties. Were you isolated, trying to bear the weight on your own? Or did you have people around you who encouraged and strengthened you? Many of us have experienced both sides—seasons of loneliness where we struggled in silence and seasons where the right people provided support, prayer, and encouragement just when we needed it most.

I remember a time when I felt overwhelmed by the pressures of stepping into my calling. Doubt crept in, and I began questioning whether I was capable of doing what God had placed in my heart. During that season, I withdrew from others, thinking I had to figure it all out alone. But it was in a moment of complete exhaustion that I finally reached out to my Pastor. Her words of encouragement, coupled with prayer and biblical wisdom, reignited my faith and reminded me that I wasn't called to do life alone. That moment reinforced the importance of surrounding myself with a godly community.

Even Jesus, though fully divine, did not walk alone. He intentionally surrounded Himself with twelve disciples, and within that group, He had an even closer circle—Peter, James, and John. If Jesus, the Son of God, valued community, how much more do we need it? Ecclesiastes 4:9-10 states: *"Two are better than one; because they have a good reward for their labor. For if they fall, the one will lift up his fellow: but woe to him that is alone when he falleth; for he hath not another to help him up."*

## Why Community Matters

- **Encouragement & Support** – In moments of doubt, the right people remind us of our calling and encourage us to keep going.

- **Accountability** – Proverbs 27:17 reminds us, *"Iron sharpeneth iron; so a man sharpeneth the countenance of his friend."* A strong community challenges us to grow.

- **Wisdom & Guidance** – God often speaks through others, providing clarity and direction when we need it most.

- **Shared Burdens & Celebrations** – Romans 12:15 reminds us, *"Rejoice with them that do rejoice, and weep with them that weep."* A strong community not only supports us through hardships but also celebrates our victories.

While solitude has its place, prolonged isolation can be detrimental to spiritual and personal growth. The enemy often seeks to attack us when we are alone, making us more vulnerable to doubt, fear, and discouragement. 1 Peter 5:8 warns us: *"Be sober, be vigilant; because your adversary the devil, as a roaring lion, walketh about, seeking whom he may devour."* When we separate ourselves from a supportive community, we make it easier for the enemy to plant seeds of doubt and discouragement in our hearts. Staying connected helps us resist these attacks and remain firm in our faith.

Think of how lions hunt in the wild—they seek out the isolated, the weak, and the unprotected. Likewise, when we separate ourselves from a supportive community, we become easier targets for the enemy's attacks. He whispers lies into our hearts: *"You're not good enough." "No one cares about you." "You're better off on your own."* But these are just tactics to keep us disconnected from the very people God has placed in our lives to help strengthen us.

There was a season in my life when I isolated myself, believing that no one could truly understand what I was going through. Instead of reaching out, I withdrew. The more I stayed in that place of solitude, the more the enemy attacked my mind. Doubt and fear crept in, and I began questioning everything—my purpose, my calling, even my worth. It wasn't until I allowed trusted friends and mentors back into my life that I found renewed strength. Their prayers, encouragement, and wisdom helped me see that I was never meant to carry my burdens alone.

Staying connected to a faith-filled community helps us resist these attacks and remain firm in our faith. Galatians 6:2 reminds us, *"Bear ye one another's burdens, and so fulfil the law of Christ."* When we have people around us who can pray for us, speak life into us, and remind us of God's promises, we gain the strength to keep pressing forward.

# How to Build a Strong Community

●**Find a Church Home:** Surround yourself with believers who encourage your spiritual growth.

●**Join a Small Group:** Bible studies, mentorship circles, or prayer groups foster deeper connections.

●**Be a Friend & Mentor:** Don't just seek community—create it. Support others in their journey as well.

●**Limit Negative Influences:** Surround yourself with those who uplift and push you toward purpose, not those who drain you.

●**Serve & Give:** True community is built through service. Look for ways to be a blessing to others, and you will find yourself surrounded by like-minded people.

The early church in Acts is a powerful example of the importance of community. Acts 2:42-47 describes how the early church flourished through fellowship. They broke bread together, prayed, and shared resources, resulting in a thriving, faith-filled community. Their unity allowed them to grow spiritually and impact the world around them. Similarly, when we invest in building strong relationships, we position ourselves for greater effectiveness in our purpose. Community is not just about receiving; it's also about giving and pouring into others. They understood that faith was not meant to be practiced in isolation, but rather, it was strengthened through relationships and shared experiences.

Imagine the first believers gathering in homes, worshiping together, and providing for one another's needs. These were people from different backgrounds, cultures, and walks of life, yet they were united by a common faith in Christ. Their bond was so strong that Acts 4:32 states, *"And the multitude of them that believed were of one heart and of one soul: neither said any of them that ought of the things which he possessed was his own; but they had all things common."* This level of unity and selflessness not only strengthened their faith but also became a testimony to others who witnessed their love for one another.

In today's world, where individualism is often celebrated, we can learn from the early church's example. Their commitment to each other was not just about social gatherings—it was about spiritual accountability, shared burdens, and mutual growth. They knew that they were stronger together, and because of their unity, they were able to spread the gospel and impact the world around them.

Similarly, when we invest in building strong relationships, we position ourselves for greater effectiveness in our purpose. Community is not just about receiving; it's also about giving and pouring into others. When we intentionally connect with others, we create a space where faith can thrive, where struggles can be shared without judgment, and where victories can be celebrated together.

If you've ever experienced a season where you felt isolated or unsupported, you know how difficult it can be to stay encouraged. But when you have a faith-filled community around you, you gain strength from their prayers, wisdom from their experiences, and confidence from their encouragement.

Think of the times in your life when someone's kindness, prayers, or encouragement lifted your spirit. Now, imagine being that person for someone else. That is the essence of community—lifting others while being lifted ourselves.

## Overcoming Challenges in Building Community

●**Fear of Vulnerability:** Being open with others can feel risky, but true community requires authenticity. Find trustworthy people who will uplift you.

●**Past Hurt or Betrayal:** Many avoid community due to past disappointments. While people are imperfect, don't allow past wounds to rob you of the blessings of godly relationships.

- **Feeling Unworthy or Unseen:** You belong in community. God has placed gifts inside of you that others need. Engage, serve, and trust that you have a role to play.

## Practical Exercise: Strengthening Your Community

- Identify one person in your life who positively influences your faith and purpose.

- Reach out to them this week with a word of encouragement or gratitude.

- If you're not part of a small group or ministry, take a step to join or start one.

By investing in godly relationships, we position ourselves to walk in our purpose with strength, accountability, and unwavering faith.

# CHAPTER 8

## WALKING IN PURPOSE

W alk in your Purpose!! Some may say this is easier said than done, but it is not. Walking in purpose is not a one-time event—it's a daily commitment. It's about aligning your actions with God's will and living a life that brings glory to Him. But what does it mean to walk in purpose, and how can you do it consistently? Considering what you have learned in the earlier chapters, you will see how easy this is. You know that walking in your Purpose requires you to allow God to lead and guide you. It requires you to adjust your thinking, think with a positive mindset, write the vision, and then work toward it. You are also required to work your Faith, not just have the Faith that things can happen for you, but to exercise that Faith, by taking the necessary steps to bring your vision to fruition. After incorporating this into your life, you will walk in your Purpose.

Your purpose is not just about what you do—it's about who you are in Christ. Ephesians 2:10 reminds us, *"For we are His workmanship, created in Christ Jesus for good works, which God prepared beforehand that we should walk in them."* In other words, God has already prepared good works for you to do. Your job is not to create your purpose, but to discover it and walk in it.

Esther's purpose was to save her people from destruction. But before she could fulfill that purpose, she had to go through a process of preparation. She didn't step into the palace overnight—her journey was marked by divine positioning, mentorship, and personal transformation. She had to learn to trust God, step out in faith, and use her position of influence for His glory. Esther's story reminds us that walking in purpose often requires courage and sacrifice.

- **Divine Positioning** – Esther didn't choose to be queen; she was chosen. She was placed in a position where her influence could be used for God's glory. Sometimes, we don't understand why God places us in certain environments, but He sees the bigger picture. Where you are right now might be part of God's preparation for your greater assignment.

- **Preparation and Growth** – Before Esther could approach the king, she had to go through a season of preparation. This represents the refining process we often go through before stepping fully into our purpose. God uses challenges, lessons, and even delays to equip us for the work ahead.

- **Courage to Act** – Esther had to take a risk. She knew that going before the king uninvited could cost her life, yet she declared, *"If I perish, I perish"* (Esther 4:16). Walking in purpose is not always comfortable—it often requires stepping out in faith, even when the outcome is uncertain.

- **Impact Beyond Herself** – Esther's purpose was not just about her personal success; it was about saving a nation. True purpose is always bigger than us. When we walk in alignment with God's plan, we become vessels for His work in the lives of others.

## Applying Esther's Story to Your Life

❖ **Where has God positioned you?** Even if you don't fully understand it yet, trust that you are where you need to be for this season.

❖ **Are you willing to go through the process?** Growth takes time, and preparation is necessary for promotion.

❖ **Will you step out in faith?** Purpose requires action, even when the future feels uncertain.

❖ **How does your purpose impact others?** Your calling is meant to glorify God and bless those around you.

Faith is essential when it comes to living out your God-given purpose. Hebrews 11:6 tells us, *"But without faith it is impossible to please him: for he that cometh to God must believe that he is, and that he is a rewarder of them that diligently seek him."* When God calls you to something greater, fear and doubt will try to hold you back. But faith allows you to move forward, trusting that He will provide, guide, and strengthen you along the way. Just like Esther, you may not have all the answers, but obedience to God's calling will always lead to a greater outcome than you could ever imagine. Purpose is not just about reaching a destination—it's about walking daily in obedience, trusting that God is leading you every step of the way.

**Practical Steps for Walking in Purpose**

❖ **Seek God Daily:** Spend time in prayer and Bible study every day. Ask God to reveal His purpose for your life. This time with God helps you tune in to His voice and allows Him to reveal His purpose for your life. Prayer is a way to express your heart, ask for guidance, and find peace in His presence. The Bible is a living word that provides wisdom, encouragement, and practical direction for your purpose.

❖ **Use Your Gifts:** Identify your spiritual gifts and talents, and look for ways to use them to serve others. Each of us has been given unique spiritual gifts and talents that align with God's purpose for our lives. It's important to recognize and cultivate these gifts, using them to serve others and bring glory to God. Your purpose is connected to the impact you have on others—whether it's teaching, encouraging, leading, or supporting—your gifts are meant to serve His kingdom.

❖ **Stay Connected:** Surround yourself with a community of believers who will encourage you, hold you accountable, and support you in your journey. God has not designed us to walk alone. Fellowship with others strengthens your faith and helps you stay focused on your purpose, especially during difficult times.

❖ **Be Intentional:** Living out your purpose requires intentionality. Make choices that align with God's calling on your life, even when they're difficult. Whether it's setting aside time for spiritual growth or making sacrifices for the greater good, intentional decisions build a life of purpose. Remember, every step you take in faith is moving you closer to fulfilling God's plan for you.

❖ **Know Who You Are**

Understanding your identity in Christ is foundational to walking in your purpose. When you know who you are—created in the image of God, loved unconditionally, and called to a divine purpose—you can walk with confidence and authority. Your purpose is not defined by your circumstances or the opinions of others; it is rooted in the truth of who God says you are.

❖ **Study the Word and Seek Godly Counsel**

The Bible is a compass for your life's journey. As you study the Word, you'll find guidance, encouragement, and wisdom that will help you navigate the challenges of fulfilling your purpose. In addition to the Word, seek counsel from wise and godly mentors who can help you discern God's will for your life.

Walking in your Purpose does not mean that everything will always go smoothly. There s the possibility of challenges, setbacks, and moments of doubt. However, the assurance we have in God is that He will never leave us, even in the toughest of times As we walk in faith, we walk knowing that God is with us—guiding, strengthening, and protecting us along the way. Remember, even in the storms, He is using everything to fulfill His purpose for your life. Walking in purpose means that you know who you are and what you are supposed to be doing on this earth and with your life. If you are walking in your God-given Purpose, you are fulfilling the will of God and bringing glory and honor to him. Whatever you have been called to do, do it with dignity, honor, respect, grace, humility, love, and in the spirit of excellence. You may face obstacles that make you question if you're on the right path. But as long as you are following God's lead, you are exactly where He wants you to be. Trust that He will provide for your needs, strengthen your heart, and direct your steps. Your journey may not look like you imagined, but it is always unfolding according to God's perfect plan. Allow your life to reflect the God that lives on the inside of you, who guides and keeps you.

Should you have a moment in your life where you feel doubtful and unsure of where you should go, you can refer to one of my favorite scriptures, which says. "For I know the thoughts that I think toward you, saith the Lord, thoughts of peace, and not of evil, to give you an expected end." (Jeremiah 29:11). God knows exactly what he wants for our lives; he wants us to be prosperous people, he wants us to have success, he wants us to enjoy the life he has given us. God does not want us to struggle, and anyone who says otherwise has not truly studied the word of God. He has given us gifts and talents to succeed in this life, but to know what they are are and how to use them to their full potential, we must seek God. Everything that he has given to us, we are to give back to him and allow these things to bring him glory. **You, yes you** that is reading this; God has greatness in store for you, and you must believe and receive it! No one can keep you from getting to where God has intended you to be but **YOU!** No one can stop your progress but **YOU!** You *must* know that you are destined for more! You *must* know that you have a purpose to fulfill in God's earthly kingdom! You must know who you are and who you belong to!

You are not just an ordinary person—you are a child of the King of kings and the Lord of lords. As His son or daughter YOU are the "lords" and the "kings" he refers to; you are ROYALTY. Stand up strong like you know who you are and why you were placed here. From this day forward you are to Walk in Your Purpose completely on Purpose! Hold your head high and know that you are a child of God and are to do his will no matter the circumstances surrounding you. When you step into your purpose, you walk in the authority and dignity that comes with your identity in Christ. You were not created to live in defeat or mediocrity. God has destined you for greatness, and no one can stop you from fulfilling His plans for your life but YOU. Be intentional in everything you do, and keep God as your head. Allow God to lead you in your way, adjust your thinking, write out your vision, work your Faith, and walk in your Purpose! Stand firm in who you are, and let your purpose shine through in everything you do. Walk in your calling with grace, humility, and excellence. Honor God with your life, and let every action, decision, and step bring glory to Him. When you walk in your purpose, you reflect the character and glory of the God who lives in you. You are here for a reason, and that reason is to fulfill the unique purpose God has placed within you.

From this day forward, choose to walk in your purpose with intentionality and confidence. Your journey is not just about reaching a destination—it's about aligning your life with God's will and trusting Him every step of the way. Keep your faith strong, seek God daily, use your gifts, and stay connected to those who will encourage and support you. Most importantly, remember that you are a child of the King. You are royal. You are equipped. You are destined for greatness. Walk in your purpose, completely on purpose, and allow God to lead the way.

Let God guide you, adjust your thinking, write your vision, and walk in faith. With God leading you, you will walk boldly On the Path to Your Purpose!

**Practical Exercise: Living on Purpose**

- Write down your top three spiritual gifts or talents.
- Identify one way you can use each gift to serve others this week.
- Pray for God's guidance as you step into your purpose.

As we come to the end of this journey, I want to leave you with a final thought: your purpose is not just about you—it's about how you can bring glory to God and impact the lives of others. Walking in purpose requires faith, action, and a willingness to let God lead. But the rewards are worth it. When you walk in purpose, you experience a sense of fulfillment and joy that can't be found anywhere else.

Remember, you are not alone on this journey. God is with you every step of the way, and He has placed people in your life to support and encourage you. Keep seeking Him, keep adjusting your thinking, and keep taking steps toward your vision. Your purpose is waiting for you—go after it with everything you've got.

Thank you for walking this **Path to Purpose** with me. Your journey of self-discovery, Faith, and fulfillment doesn't have to end here. If you're looking for more inspiration and guidance, I invite you to explore my other works:

- **The Path to Purpose Reflection Guide**
- **Dear Woman of God**

- **The Graced. Restored. Transformed. Planner**

Visit www.sufficientlycovered.com to learn more and grab your copies today!

**The Path to Purpose Reflection Guide**

Designed to be your personal space for reflection, growth, and a deeper connection with God. With guided prompts, thought-provoking questions, and space to capture your prayers and revelations, this journal will help you apply the lessons from the book to your daily life.

**Dear Woman of God**

A heartfelt and empowering book written to encourage women in their Faith, Purpose, and personal growth. Dear Woman of God, reminds you that you are seen, loved, and chosen.

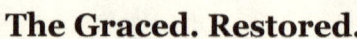 **The Graced. Restored. Transformed. Planner**

This **faith-based planner** is designed to help you stay organized while nurturing your spiritual and personal growth. With guided reflections, goal-setting tools, and scripture-based affirmations, it's more than just a planner—a space to walk boldly in grace and transformation.

"Don't count yourself out; there is always room to improve. When you look in the mirror, know that you are the child of a King, and he wants you to be prosperous. There is nothing or no one that can stop you except YOU! Be all that God has said you are; do all that God has said you can do. Don't stop until God calls you home! You have greatness in you; let it shine!"

**With Purpose & Grace,**

*Tranisha LeShawn*